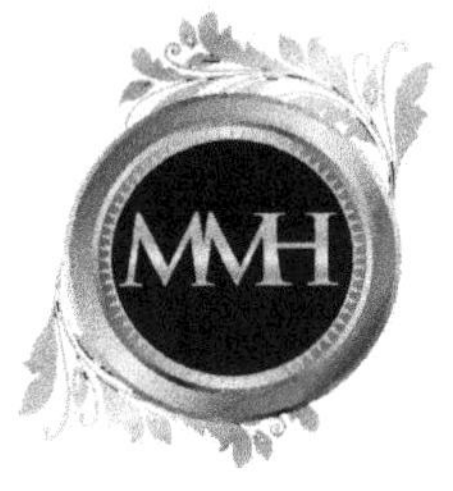


# Become Your Own PUBLISHER

KAREN MC DERMOTT

Making Magic Happen books may be ordered through online booksellers or by contacting:

makingmagichappenpublishing@gmail.com



ISBN: (sc) 978-0-9946337-5-0

ISBN: (e) 978-0-9946337-6-7

# Dedication

To those special people who are brave enough to pursue their life's purpose.

*'Share your story and you may inspire another'*

# Foreword

So many people dream about becoming authors and that magical day when they'll see their book in a bookshop, but for so many people this dream remains exactly that, a 'dream'. The task can seem so daunting and overwhelming, there are so many unknowns and so many questions ... but not anymore.

This book is filled with everything you need to know to get you started on your journey to becoming a published author!

Karen has helped teach hundreds of people how to publish their books and now she brings this knowledge together to help many more. She loves writing and encouraging people to not be afraid to share their story. Karen is especially passionate about inspiring people to make magic happen in their lives and I'm so delighted that you've taken the step to create magic in yours by reading this book.

Peace Mitchell

Founder

The Women's Business School

www.thewomensbusinessschool.com

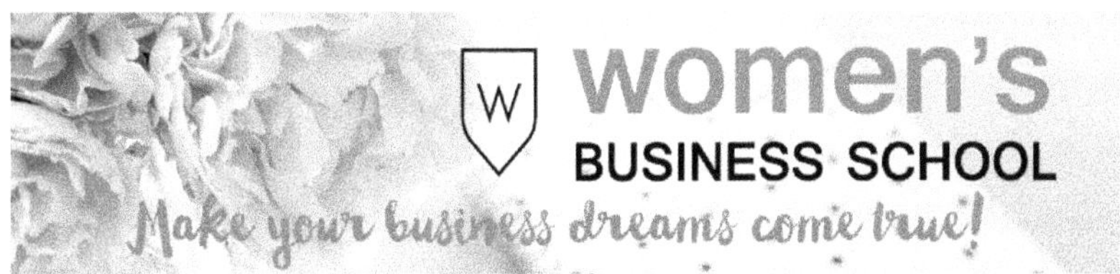

# *Contents*

# *Introduction*

IF you have purchased this book, then I will be bold and presume that you are planning on publishing a book in the not too distant future.

Yes? Great. Let's get started.

In this guide you will learn how to get your book written, edited, published, marketed, and lots of other things that I have learnt along the way. When you enter this industry you will never be bored because the landscape is forever changing. There is always lots to do to learn, improve and move forward.

It excites me to sit down and write a non-fiction book. My genre of choice is fiction, nevertheless I have years of experience in this industry and have been an integral part of the success of Serenity Press. I have also been actively writing blog posts since 2009. These have been picked up for publication in magazines, books and online. For the past year I have been sharing my knowledge of publishing through the Ausmumpreneur network as their publishing expert. This network is the number one place to be for Australian women in business.

Publishing has changed and is no longer an unattainable dream. Yes, it is fabulous to be offered a contract with a big-name publisher who can place your book on every bookshelf, but in reality if you have not made waves in the literary scene beforehand, do not have a direct link inside the industry or a huge following, then the chance of that happening is minute.

So what I would like to say is ...why not become your own publisher?

Authors have to work increasingly hard to raise their profile to assist their publishers sell books. Who do you think is going to make the most out of each book sale? The publisher of course! Rightly so, as they are the ones taking the financial risk on your book.

When you enter the publishing industry, it is amazing the wealth of knowledge out. In writing this book, it is my intention for you to gain enough knowledge and inspiration from my journey to apply it directly to successfully building your own publishing empire. There is enough room for us all in this world.

# *Building your Brand*

Building your brand – when do you start?

This subject is so important, especially if you want to sell books. Most big-name authors spend a lot of time building and promoting their brand to build a rapport with their readers. If you are in business, you may already have an established audience, so you are a step ahead.

Your brand is what people first experience when they interact with you (if you are the actual brand) or your business. Every experience, product, hearsay, interaction or anything associated with your brand has an impact on the empire you are creating. I was not always fully aware of this while building the Serenity Press brand. And yes, I made mistakes. However, I work hard to turn mistakes around in my favour. If you are aware of what to do from the start, then you are one step ahead already.

There will, of course, always be room to grow and expand

your brand. But imagine if you got it right, at the beginning of your journey.

***Here are some tips to consider:***

***Design:*** It makes a positive impact if your brand design is targeted toward the clientele you are hoping to attract. If design is not your strong point, then investing in this is definitely worth it. Think of it like a book cover. People are more likely to pick up and consider buying your book if they are attracted to it. Appealing to your niche is paramount at this stage.

Your logo is important. It is benefits from being instantly identifiable and triggers a 'must have' emotional endorphin rush in your target consumer.

***Mindfulness:*** People don't necessarily remember all details, but they will remember how they feel about certain books, products and services they have acquired. Focus some energy on ensuring you provide the emotional experience you hope to promote.

Every interaction you have, no matter how small, has the potential to build or damage your brand. Always aim for a best-case scenario.

***Give more:*** I am a giving person by nature. I feel good when I give someone something they really desire. I have become a publisher because I love to give authors the dream of holding their book in their hands. I guide them through the often daunting process of publishing, and as you learn, you may consider doing the same. Karma is a wonderful thing in business.

***Inspire:*** I have experienced firsthand the potential power words have in helping someone move forward, feeling supported and not alone. If you offer a service or product, give that little extra. It may make a big difference.

***Helping others:*** Often the work I do out of the goodness of my heart leads to amazing affiliations, partnerships and sales, such as taking on community or charity projects. I do this with no expectation from the project, other than to make something magical happen for those in need because this is important to me and makes my heart sing. Quite often the most amazing things find their way back to me through my act of kindness. It is important that if you choose to give, you do not expect to receive in return. Give with an open heart and the best of intention.

***Integrity:*** Be that business people want to be part of; be the success story and defy odds. Be true to your values and principles as they are hard to retrieve once they are gone.

As you build your brand your business will evolve, your worth will increase and you will grow and bring more people or services on board. Grow at the organic speed of your business; don't push too hard, but be prepared to work hard when things are moving fast. It will all balance out. If your business keeps growing at a steady pace, it may be good to consider taking on a partner or some staff to help you out.

***Plant seeds:*** Inspiration is a gift and, when pursued with passion, wonderful things can grow. Be brave, be innovative and be kind to yourself – it's going to be hard work.

***Hard work and focus:*** People often admire others who work hard to achieve goals. Let's be honest, some people get lucky, but building, growing and sustaining a business is hard work and requires a lot of determination and focus. Nurture those seeds.

***Partnerships:*** Partnering and affiliating with complementary brands and services is an amazing way to build your brand.

When two businesses complement each other, clicking in place like jigsaw pieces, amazing things can happen for everyone involved. I love it when amazing people come together.

***Treasure your tribe:*** Since joining the Ausmumpreneur network, my opportunities have increased tenfold. Being a mother and building a business at the same time can be quite isolating and limiting, but in this fabulous community there are no obstacles to achieving everything you want for your business.

When I joined the network I had no expectations of making big sales or the amazing friendships and contacts I would establish. I am so proud that my hard-working and caring nature has been recognised and embraced wholly by this amazing group of women who lift each other up every day.

I advise you to find a strong network of like-minded people to help you move forward in your business. I was becoming a bit rigid until I did this. By surrounding myself with other successful businesses and businesswomen, I was introduced to the ways they 'made it'. I realsied I wasn't fluffing my way through my business – I was actually doing well and if I implemented some structures and a more strategic business plan I would attract the type of financial backing I needed to be a successful business. I will talk more about this in a future chapter.

In summary, putting some time into building your brand from the beginning is important. Serenity Press has recently rebranded because we have changed towards a more traditional publishing model.

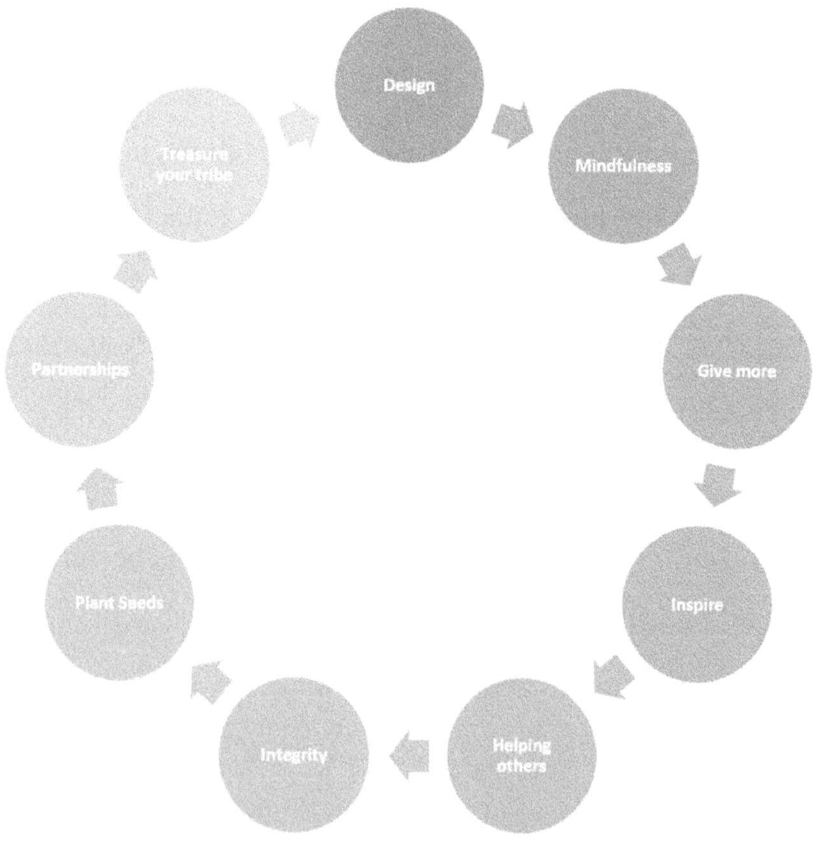

# *Writing your book*

If you have not yet written your book this chapter is written with the intention of inspiring and guiding you through the process.

I like to keep things simple and write through my heart. Recently I have also been incorporating my head in the process and the two make a winning combination. Now to

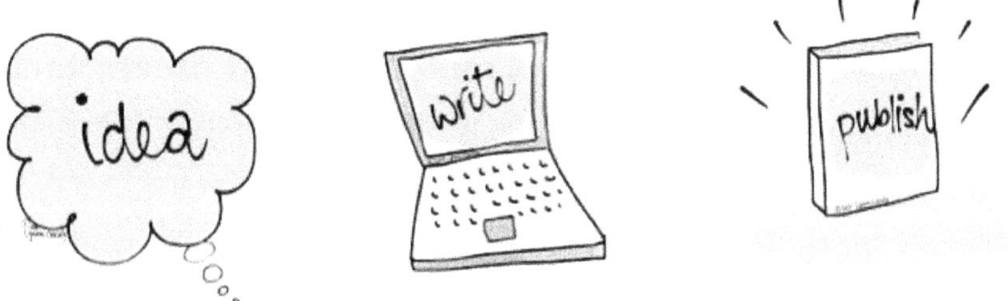


Writing: The process

I have worked with many authors, and being an author myself, I have realised that taking shortcuts is often not the best practice. When I began writing, I was totally disillusioned about the process I have now come to respect wholeheartedly.

I thought that when I wrote a book, that was the hard bit over! Sorry to burst the bubble, but it is just the beginning and that is why so many people don't make it. It was not necessarily a bad thing – sometimes ignorance is bliss. I liken it to having a baby (and I have had six). When you first get pregnant it is all romantic, but the pregnancy can be tough or smooth sailing … and it takes time. The birth is painful, whether it is natural or surgical, but it is oh-so-worth-it when you hold that bundle of joy in your arms.  And to think you would undertake it all again …

There are plenty of people out there who can help you make your book the best it can be at a high price, but I feel it is important for the author to be more involved in how their book evolves.

If you want to do it right it is important to follow the process.

Think: Get your thoughts down on paper and be creative. Your book wants you to write it. Write down everything you can think of and put it in some sort of order.

Jot down potential chapters, then scenes and characters for

fiction (or content if you are writing self-help or non-fiction). I don't stress if what I am writing is not perfect. At this stage my focus is on getting down as much as I can. Research can be carried out during the preparation stage, but don't limit yourself to this you may find that researching is a running theme throughout.

Writing your book is the action part of the process. You are getting words onto paper. It is not the time to worry, but to get writing and see where your story takes you. If you need to check something or come back to a scene, highlight a note in red within your document and return to it when you can.

Once you have your book written, what a great feeling it is. You want to celebrate and shout to the world: 'I have written a book! Here it is!' But it is important to be realistic and know that it is not ready to go out into the world quite yet. By all means, post the exciting news on social media that you have completed your first draft and share it with your loved ones. You deserve to celebrate as you have completed something that many people abandon.

The next steps are what will separate you from the amateurs. Do the hard work now and you will not regret it.

My advice is to put your book baby away for two weeks and revisit it with a clear mind. Then read it through and self-edit it as you go along, without being too harsh. When you have accomplished that stage you could ask a 'beta reader' to look over it for you. This could be another author or someone you respect who is willing to do this for you. Having a beta reader is always a great idea. They will want the best for your book and will invest their time and energy in providing feedback on content, flow and if they enjoyed your book. They will probably also create some anticipation for you on social media.

Perfectionism is wonderful but don't let it build a wall, blocking you from moving forward. This process is used by many successful authors, so don't be disheartened.

Consider the advice that your beta reader has provided, take on board what you know needs enhancing ... and then it is time to edit ...

# *Editing*

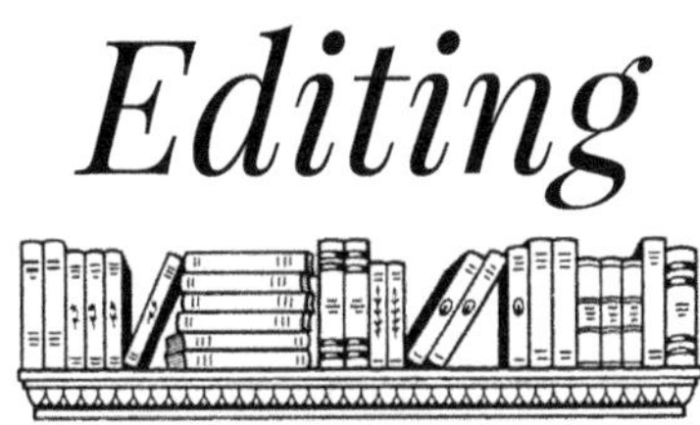

Editing is one of the most important aspects of completing your book. It can also be one of the most tedious stages. The level of editing required will depend on your writing skills. Even if you feel that you are not a good editor, I advise you to go over your manuscript at least twice. Firstly, as a reader to check the flow of your book. Secondly, to correct any typos and grammatical issues.

Working through those stages is wonderful and makes your manuscript stronger. Again, sorry to be the bearer of bad news, but this does not necessarily mean your manuscript is ready to go to print.

It is important that you make your work the best it can be, so at this stage you can outsource to an editor. There are some amazing editors in the Ausmumpreneur Network who are trustworthy and will provide you with an honest assessment of your manuscript.

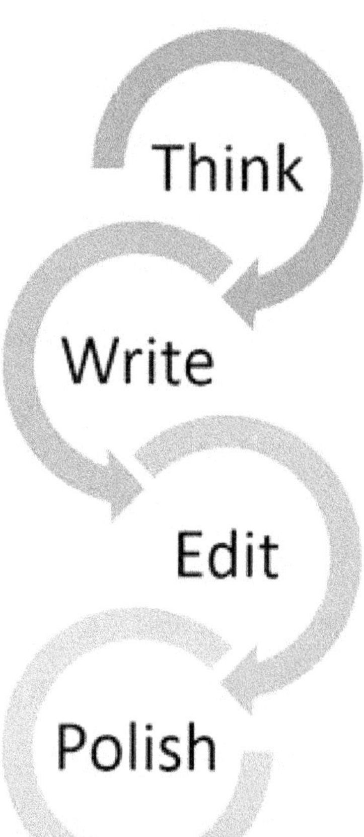
Think
Write
Edit
Polish

If you only plan to write one book, you might not feel the need to upskill your editing skills, however if you do intend to write more books it is a worthwhile investment. Many of us feel time poor in this busy business world, but my advice is not to cut corners on editing.

***My top editing tips are:***

- Go through your manuscript with different editing caps on
- Stay positive during the editing process
- It's great to find a way that works for you
- Be proud – all of your hard work will pay off
- Know that your book is the best it can be. will provide you with the confidence needed to promote it and see it become a best seller with an abundance of five-star reviews.

Editing is so important and published books are edited many times before they make it to the shelves.

# *Publishing your Book*

The landscape of publishing has changed over the past few years. Many authors have altered their perspective on how traditional publishing is perceived. Self-publishing is no longer frowned upon as it once was. There are now many self-published authors consciously choosing to be in control, and by connecting with their inner entrepreneur they are doing really well. This is great news for aspiring authors. You no longer need to sit around hoping that a traditional publisher will send you a publishing offer rather than a rejection. You can take positive action towards publishing your own book. This is an ideal scenario for action-based entrepreneurs.

***A little about my journey***

When I began writing, I aspired to be a successful author. I self-published my first novel and it was a negative experience, however through that experience I learnt the process of publishing a book. Time and circumstance aligned and I was ready to act when opportunity arose and so my journey has continued to where I find myself today. My inner entrepreneur didn't feel happy clinging onto a small hope that my book might be 'picked up' by a publisher. I chose to take positive action to work towards my dream. I knew it may take time to perfect but I was open and excited to learn new things. In doing so I could also help others publish their books in a positive way and collect stories for inspiring anthologies. If I can do it, so can you.

I am going to chat about three options for you as an author:

1. Self-publishing.
2. Traditional publishing.
3. eBook publishing

# *Self-Publishing*

You have written a book and chosen to self-publish it. What do you do?

As a self-publishing author it is up to you to make sure your book is as good as it can be. It's all well and good to write a book and publish it, but ensuring the quality is equal to that of a traditionally published book is the key to making your book saleable. I highly recommend self-editing and if you can afford it, professional editing, or at least a proofread.

There are many platforms you can use to publish your book. CreateSpace (owned by Amazon) and IngramSpark (owned by Ingram Content Group) are two of the most popular. Through these platforms your book will be available worldwide in print and eBook formats. You will need to have your files prepared and ready for uploading in pdf format for print and epub for eBook. Both platforms have plenty of guidance on how to publish with them so it is worthwhile taking some time to learn. It is a cost effective way to publish your book and reach your readership.

You will discover that setup fees are quite similar no matter whether you have a 400-page novel or a 22-page children's book. CreateSpace is very popular with authors because there is no charge for revisions and everything is quite automatic. They have a template you can load into and lots of advice on how to make your book visually appealing.

Living in Australia, I suggest you consider IngramSpark as they have an office and printing house in Melbourne. They print black and white books through there and you can have them quite fast if need be, and even pick them up yourself if you are Melbourne-based. They do print colour through their printing house partners in the UK and America. There is also an option to rush both production and shipping. This option is priceless when you have a deadline, but it is important to remember that it does cost extra. If you need a colour print run it is commissioned through their US printing house. They do not charge you the extra shipping costs, but it will take at least three weeks to receive your order so plan well ahead.

We use the Lightning Source division of Ingram for our print-on-demand (POD) titles. I suggest you create an account with them if you aspire to having your own publishing press. They are recognised by bookstores, which is important when you are in the business.

All in all, you can publish your book quite inexpensively yourself and have it available globally through online retailers. If you would only like to have your book available as a Kindle eBook, you can do this by creating an account through KDP Select. My advice is to upload your manuscript in Word format as it will transfer better. For children's books, I suggest you download the Kindle Kids Book Creator. You can upload your pdf file and it will be transformed into a .mobi file, perfect for Kindle.

There are numerous self-publishing businesses ready to publish your book straight away. There are costs involved, all differing depending on the level of service you require. You really can do it yourself but if it is overwhelming or you don't have the time or computer skills required, it is advantageous to source assistance.

- Do your homework to find the right assistance for you
- Costs can vary considerably so be mindful who you choose.

# *Traditional publishing*

Having a big-name publisher take on your book is a dream scenario for many authors. You will not have the control or commission from each sale that self-publishing offers, but you will have an established market ready to buy your book.

If you approach a publisher and they reject your manuscript, it is important to remember it is not always a reflection of the quality of your work. It could be a case of your book not fitting with their publishing schedule at that time, or your book could be similar to another that has already been accepted. There are a number of people at a publishing house involved in the decision about whether to take on a new title. Sometimes a manuscript will go to an acquisitions meeting, but the publisher cannot convince the sales and marketing team to say yes. The best way to secure a publisher is through a literary agent who will know what each publisher is looking for at any given time. However it is not an easy feat to secure an agent.

One way to draw attention to yourself is to demonstrate how well you will sell your books, and this means getting yourself 'out there'. If you are in have a big online following, you should have a better chance of securing a deal with a publisher.

It is worth noting that you will receive a smaller percentage of sales, however your workload will be greatly reduced if your book is traditionally published opposed to self-publishing.

There are many advantages to publishing a book, especially if it complements your business or fits in with a popular genre. You will also gain instant credibility as many people aspire to become an author, often perceiving it to be an unachievable goal. Attracting the attention of the media is more successful when you are an author.

The purpose of this book is for you to consider becoming your own publisher and whether the benefits of self-publishing outweigh those of being with one of the 'big five' publishers.

# eBooks

eBooks can be used to your advantage while publishing a book. In fact, some eBook publishers focus solely on eBook distribution which cuts out significant production costs, however it doesn't cut out editing.

Direct book sales are where you will make the most per book income. However there are a lot of customers out there with ready access to their electronic reading devices who can access your book instantly when they come across it, are in contact with you or if you are recommended to them. Readers who love their electronic reading device will rarely buy a print copy unless it is at an author event and they can get it signed.

Another thing to keep in mind is to keep your title at a reasonable price. You won't make bestseller status by having your eBook listed for $9.99 if you are largely unknown. Best-selling novelists will get away with this on the book's release as demand is high and readers are willing to invest in the writer. If that is not the case for you I would suggest modest pricing for your eBook.

Amazon has an option to check the recommended pricing for your type of book so I suggest utilising that if you are going with KDP. Your book should be approved overnight with KDP.

While Amazon is a major eBook distributer, they are not the only company offering this service. Kobo and iTunes also sell eBooks. IngramSpark have a good low-cost eBook distribution service. One file set up and your title is distributed to the major eBook sellers, so it is definitely worth considering.

If your goal is to become a renowned author with a strong loyal readership, following these steps will help you build a strong platform on which to grow.

eBook success

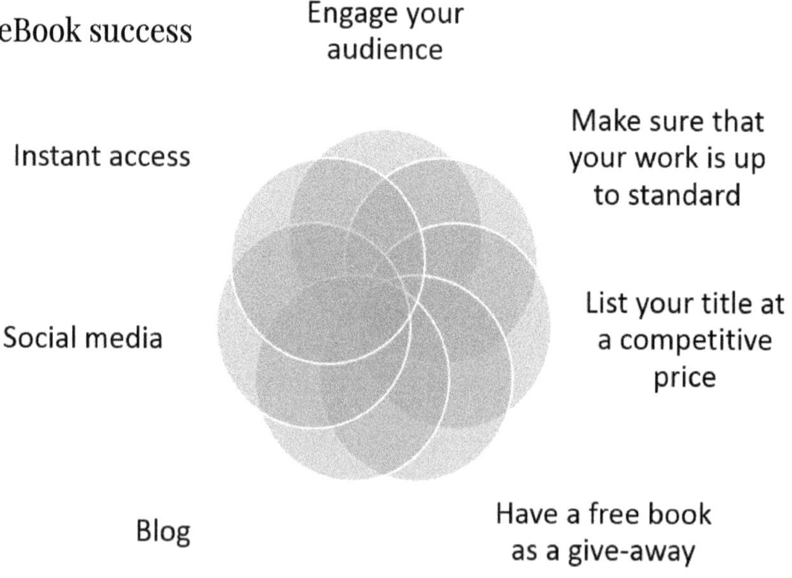

# *Selling Books*

You have published your book and now want to get it into the hands of every possible reader. How do you do it?

I have learnt so much about selling books this past few months since focusing my intention on distribution for 2016.

There are many ways of selling your book. The diagram below displays available options

Through POD (Print on Demand), eBooks, direct to customer, bulk orders and wholesale distribution.

POD

eBook

Direct to customer

Bulk pre-order sales

Wholesale Distribution

### *POD (Print on demand)*

POD is a fabulous way to publish your book with minimal financial commitment and risk. If you have an established readership, you are one major step ahead and I would suggest a more commercial approach to sales. However POD still will have its place in servicing global customers.

With POD you can have your book available through worldwide distribution. This means your files will be available to print in printing houses situated in different locations across the globe to service your readers internationally. Customers will be able to source your title through a leading online book store; the order will be processed without you having to do a thing. Alternatively, a customer may order a book through you and you can process it on your account with your printing/ distribution company (IngramSpark, CreateSpace, Lightning Source).

Shipping orders internationally from Australia can be costly, so as it is cheaper to set up files through these distribution channels even if you have printed a bulk order to be stored in your warehouse I would still recommend this option for overseas orders. (However, specialised printing is limited).

POD is also a really productive way to get your book published and then pursue media attention, distributors etc. Once they have a tangible product in their hands it is easier for them to say yes than if they just have a concept.

### *Catalogues*

It is beneficial to have your book displayed in catalogues alongside other books in your genre, whether direct to the customer or a book buyer. There are many different catalogues out there so find where your title fits and try to have it included.

### *Schools and Libraries*

Libraries and schools buy a lot of books. Each state will have its own sales direct representative for schools and libraries. In Western Australia it is Westbooks. The key is to liaise with them and arrange an appointment. Have your book catalogued with the National Library of Australia with an ISBN and have a copy of your book stocked there. James Bennett is also a direct library supplier and they have a link to Booktopia.

### *Bookstores*

To see your book stocked on a bookshelf is something very

special for every author; it is the ultimate dream. This is possible for self-published authors but is unlikely unless you have a big following or a distribution company. You will need to think and invest like a publishing house to make it happen. It is important to remember that you will be the one taking the financial risk, not the retailer.

Here is an example of how you can make it happen. Firstly, it is advised that you reduce the cost of your book production to enable to you to make a profit. Working with distributors and bookstores can really eat into your profits, which allows the bookstore leverage for a competitive price on your title while making money themselves.

Many direct to store distributors are closed to individual accounts, however it is still worth asking. Novella Distribution is a new distributor who is active in getting books out to stores, into schools and distributed generally. They tell you how many books they expect to sell, you send them to them on consignment and receive a monthly record of sales.

Another option is to research sales representatives who introduce books in your genre to stores. When you approach them it is advisable to have a strong pitch explaining why they should add your book to their schedule.

Titlepage is a database where bookstores in Australia and New Zealand often go to source titles in specific genres. The key to capitalising here is to have your book categorised correctly. If you are confused contact them, they are very happy to help.

Working with bookstores individually in your local area is fine but it takes a lot of time. They want a high percentage of profits, often up to 45 percent of recommended retail price (RRP) and distributors will want more than that, often up to 70 percent.

You will also be requested to place books there on consignment and chasing payments is never a nice thing to do. In my experience and in feedback from authors who have pursued this path, it has always ended up being a costly time-consuming venture. This is not to say that with the right focus and contacts you won't be successful in supplying directly to individual stores.

It is my hope that you channel your time and energy to the most productive sales channel for your book.

### *Big Buyers*

Did you know that there are big buyers who see books at least five months in advance? Getting big buyers on board is wonderful as it will pay for a large overseas print run, however it is good to be mindful that they will require up to 70% off RRP which is quite a put-off but if you are thinking big, you will be thinking books on shelves and in homes so it is most definitely worth it.

### *eBook distribution*

The main eBook sellers are Amazon Kindle, Barnes & Noble and iBooks. You can set up files directly to each of these platforms or utilise your account through IngramSpark, who service all three retailers. They do require that you have your files in epub format.

Amazon Kindle's KDP platform is easy to manage. The format to upload to this platform is Word and for your children's books you can use their Kindle Kids Book Creator as it turns your files easily into .mobi files. It is easy to manage offers and there is a helpful price setting section in the setup process. Sales are easy to monitor on your account also, so you can gauge what campaigns are most effective.

The key to achieving sales in eBooks is to have your book not too highly priced, have effective keywords in place and encourage readers to review your book. Be proactive in promoting your eBook. There are lots of eBook readers in the world and you need to make your eBook stand out from the crowd so that reader will press the buy button.

You can now set your eBook up on pre-order for presales in anticipation of a launch, and it will be delivered to your customer's reading device on release day.

Best seller status is highly achievable with eBooks. This often happens through a promotional discount period and when partnered with influencers in your genre or a widely anticipated launch. It is important that your book is categorised for success so take some time in placing it in the right category during setup.

The cover is a major selling point so if you are not a savvy cover designer it is best to hire a professional as it is important to make your book visually appealing to your customer.

## *Give to receive*

When you are marketing your book in anticipation of its launch it is most definitely worth compiling a list of influencers to receive gifts of your book. In the publishing world these books are called Advanced Reading Copies (ARCs) and are important to stimulate interest before release. Connect with these influencers and try to have them agree to read your book before you send it. If the right person promotes your book at the right time, magic happens.

Many of our individual sales waves come when someone with a strong social media presence promotes your book.

### *Bulk sales*

If you are a big thinker then you should focus some energy on securing bulk orders.

If you have a big social media following or a very strong partnership with an influencer who is willing to promote your book, focusing energy into a big pre-order campaign is the way to go. This way you will secure enough sales to make bulk print viable and you cut out the middle men in the process. The reality is that there is a lot of work in processing orders so that is something to be mindful of.

Focusing energy in targeting a bulk order from a business that is interested in your genre of book is also a very smart move. I have seen many authors successfully secure contracts to supply bulk orders for their titles. Again, you would mould your pitch to suit the business you are approaching.

Bulk sales are a great way to achieving Best Selling order status. This is a great accolade to have when hosting events and public speaking appearances, which in turn are also great opportunities to capitalise on sales. Readers love to meet the author and have their book personally signed, or alternatively you could have them pre-signed for sales throughout the event without having to be there.

This leads me onto the option of a book tour. If your book is commercial enough it is worth considering a book tour. This can be a costly exercise and often authors team up and visit a few major cities where readers will come to meet and greet. It is also an investment in yourself if you are hoping to publish future books and create a following. Readers love to know their author.

### *Commercial distribution*

Finding the right distributor can be challenging but it is not impossible. Distributors want to sell books – that's how they make an income. Get yourself best prepared to be accepted by having a strong marketing campaign in place. Ensure your book is the best quality you can at minimal cost to you, ensuring that you can capitalise on this. Think like a publisher!

It is important to note that return per book is not much when supplying to distributors, sometimes as low as 30 percent of RRP. But the capacity to sell books is dramatically increased so it is up to you to determine if you are prepared to take a risk.

Woodslane is an approachable distribution company based in Sydney. You can register with them and have your book stocked in their warehouse if they take you on. You can stock 100 copies or 1000, depending on how big your marketing campaign will be. I talked with an inside contact who informed me that you can expect to typically sell 200 books with a small marketing campaign and 1200 or more with a national campaign. It is also good to know they have Big W on their portfolio.

New South books are another big distributor for publishing houses, but are closed to taking on new accounts at present. Their distribution house is TPL Distribution so it may be worth pursuing an account with them.

There are lots of different ways to sell your book. Take some time to sit down and work out exactly what is the right blend for your book.

### *A few tips to sales success*

1. Do your research

2. Undertake relevant marketing, marketing and more marketing;

3. Find out who the big publishing houses use to distribute in your genre and contact them directly;

4. Pursue the big sales opportunities –

that can be a single wave of sales or bulk sales;

5. Build your brand.

Research.

Marketing, marketing and more marketing.

Contact popular distributors.

Pursue the big sales opportunities.

Keep building your brand.

I do wish for high sales volumes for us all. We all have so much to share with each other and a book filled with priceless, precious information is a minimal investment with high potential for each reader. This should not be under-valued; it should be treasured.

There is enough room for multiple best-selling books in this world so let's not compete with each other. I suggest we elevate each other. Some of the best-selling romance authors that I know all support each other; they have an amazing tribe of followers who are keen to discover a new amazing talent.

This year I am delighted to be a part of the Small Press Network (SPN) distribution subcommittee. This proactive group of small publishers have banded together to make a positive difference in getting books onto store shelves and increasing sales for the smaller publishers. Watch this space.

# *Marketing*

Knowing how to market your book is really important in creating a hype about an impending release. You can take advantage of pre-sales and your book will hopefully fly off the shelves on release.

I have heard that it takes someone to see something seven times before it leaves an imprint on their memory. Logically, this makes complete sense and indicates that you should have your book displayed everywhere your target audience may be.

- Press release
- Create a stir in social media
- AusRom Today publicity
- Giveaways (facebook, goodreads, romance pages, twitter etc)
- Encouraged authors to promote.
- Instagram campaign
- Front page on release day
- First 100 copies signed and numbered.

Market a book well and watch as it takes off. It doesn't have to cost a fortune, however adopting strategic planning is important.

A marketing plan should be specific for each book although the most important core principles of marketing can be the same and enhanced accordingly.

The following is an example of how we marketed a romance anthology featuring six authors we launched in November last year.

The book was set in our hometown and we wanted to get people talking about it because of its local setting. We made the front page of one of the local papers!

# Building your business

*Partnerships, business knowledge and memberships*

If you hope your publishing business will grow, regardless of whether you are just publishing your own books or have taken the plunge to publish or represent others, it is important to be part of a community of supportive business individuals who will inspire you to think bigger and take informed risks.

When you move forward surrounded by supportive people it is less likely that you will make mistakes. Have a clear vision, know what it is you want to acheive and go after it with gusto. Your awareness will guide you to where you need to be at any given time, step by step so that you will not become overwhelmed. When opportunity arises grasp it with both hands! Knowing what opportunities to embrace will be based on your instinct and the knowledge you have accumulated thus far. You may need to push past some boundaries to acheive your goals so do it at a pace you are comfortable with.

***Position yourself so that when that big deal comes, you are ready to deliver!***

# *What do you believe?*

I was recently a panellist at the Women's Business School in Perth, which was hosted by the amazing Peace and Katy from Ausmumpreneur. They invited me to join them for the whole day and it was an amazing experience. We worked through lots of amazing business enhancing exercises and I learnt lots. I was challenged outside my comfort zone in a safe way and it worked wonders. I left feeling so excited about the new directions Serenity Press is taking, and even though I am taking on some huge projects I am excited about each of them. This is largely because of the support, encouragement and knowledge I receive from the Ausmumpreneur network. Thinking big isn't as frightening as it could potentially have been.

When business is broken down into small steps it doesn't seem such a huge endeavour.

During the day we were asked to partner with someone to share our three Whys. These are the essence of what we believe in and gift us with our heart-centred goal for our business. Our passion, our drive and our enthusiasm comes from these core beliefs so this exercise is simple, yet very powerful when embraced whole-heartedly.

***My three beliefs are:***

***1. I believe we all can make magic happen.***

***2. I believe we all can have a positive impact on each other's lives.***

***3. I believe in the power of the written word.***

When the third belief flowed through me and out of my mouth it came with such intensity that my partner went 'Wow'. I knew she felt the energy that was emitted with each word. So when everyone was asked to share their beliefs – and with a little nudge in my back from my partner – I said, 'I believe in the power of the written word.' Again, gasps – these words that came straight from my heart-centred core were having the impact I had hoped for.

It was through writing my first book The Visitor that I learnt how effective writing with this energy is. Every word in that book was penned through the same heart-centred intensity.

I have had many people connect with me saying they don't know exactly why, but the book had reached into their hearts and given them the answer they longed for.

I know without a shadow of a doubt that it is the same energy I founded Serenity Press with. Every endeavour I pursue using this magic attracts the most beautiful people my way. Unexpected things happen and everything falls into place just as it should be. It is a very fulfilling feeling to know the business you created through your heart-centred goal, with not much more than the knowing feeling you were doing the right thing, is embraced by the people you hoped to embrace.

Serenity Press has turned the page and started a new chapter. Amazing things are happening in a big way, with an amazing heart-centred team supporting us. We are grateful, we are ambitious and we are excited. We are determined to make a difference by creating publishing opportunities for authors. We are here for the long haul, with strong foundations in place that we are hard at work building upon to create our empire.

All of this has been possible because of unwavering belief. I believe, and through the actions I take instigated through that belief, others begin to believe too. When you are part of an uplifting group of like-minded people like the Ausmumpeneur network and with the support we have from the amazing Australian writer community

We hope that you find the same for your business and your heart-centred goal.

What do you believe?

*I beleieve* ______________________________

# *Heart Writing can be good for business*

Writing articles is a wonderful way of building a relationship with clients and people interested in what you have to offer. Putting a lot of information on a page may leave someone informed but have you given the best of you? Have you truly engaged and connected with them?

The articles I write through heart writing are the ones that get the most positive comments and are read more widely. Why? Because it is obvious that I am authentic and willing to share myself with my readers, therefore I connect on a deeper level.

This type of connection is important as it is like a tattoo imprinting into your reader's heart and mind. They will be willing to invest in what you have to offer if they feel a connection. They will remember how you made them feel and therefore they may seek other articles you have written which may lead them to books, workshops and services that you may have on offer. This is the highest form of engagement when building your profile. People will want to remember you and talk about you to their friends and groups.

People will always remember how you made them feel.

I have watched many people build their profiles through heart writing. It is a positive if you are resilient and only focus on what your intention may be. It is important to be mindful that you are not going to please everyone.

When you engage the right person/audience, then your platform will expand, and before you know it you will have a wider audience than ever before. It is your job to ensure you are ready for that to happen. When sudden growth takes place it can be really overwhelming if you are not prepared for it, so always think big. (I will chat about that in another article)

I believe in the power of the written word. This is one of my core beliefs. I am truly passionate about it and when I write I open my heart; the words just flow out. My first novel was written directly through this channel and it still conjures up all kinds of emotions in people. The connections I am proudest of are the ones where, through my words, people found comfort in their time of grief. Others have found hope and others heard words of wisdom. All readers vary.

For a number of years, I wrote for a website called Building Beautiful Bonds. It was at a time when I was experiencing huge personal growth. My articles were read more than 56,000 times so I knew that I was engaging with people. We did not promote the site or articles at all so this was a triumph. I have recently compiled the main articles into a book I called Heart Writer.

It is now deemed a strength to share your challenges. It gives your profile more depth. There is no need to hide behind a screen. Stepping out and sharing your 'why' is a very powerful way to attract people to your business. I regularly share my experiences and people who take the time to connect with me discover that I am a very passionate, driven person who has a heart-centred passion for everything she endeavours.

So the next time you are writing an article or sharing your business story, consider putting some heart into it. It could end up being one of your best investments.

# Blogging

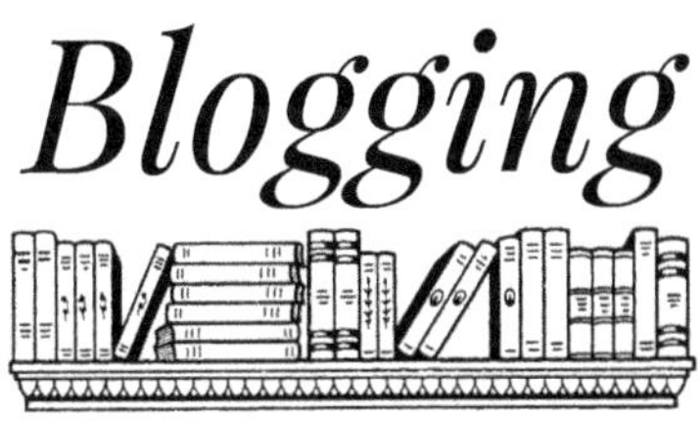

Blogging is a good way to build an audience and build your brand. Your readers will get to know you and a relationship of trust will already have been established. Your readers will also be familiar with your style of writing and won't think twice about investing in your book.

Blogging does take time and commitment though. Readers will want to read something from you pretty regularly and you should aim for at least one blog a week to build momentum.

Here are some benefits to blogging:

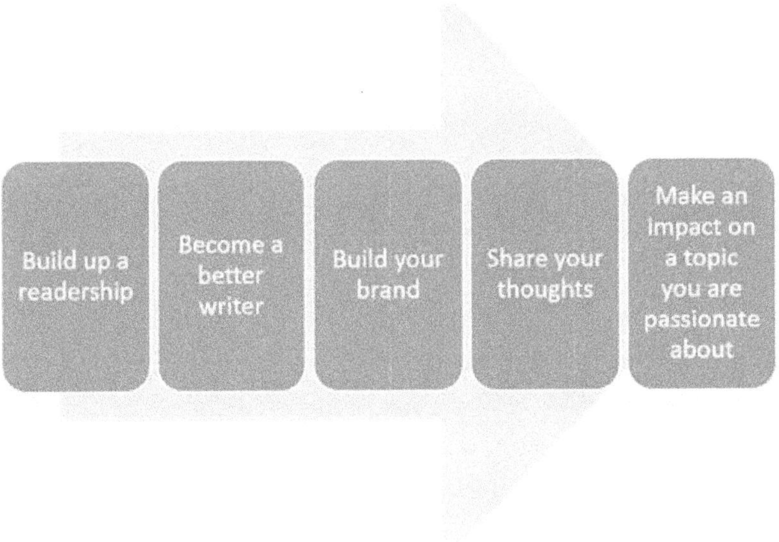

You can connect a blog to your website which will drive traffic through your point of sale. That is always a good thing, especially if your website is visually appealing to your niche market.

# *Website*

Having a website is not compulsory these days as a lot of activity happens on social media platforms.

However, it is advised to have a visually appealing website. Why? Because often interested parties will go to your website to find out more about you. It is also a one-stop place that can hold all of your important information in one place without potential clients having to scroll down news feeds.

Imagine if you lost a huge opportunity because you didn't have a website.

What you should consider when setting up your website:

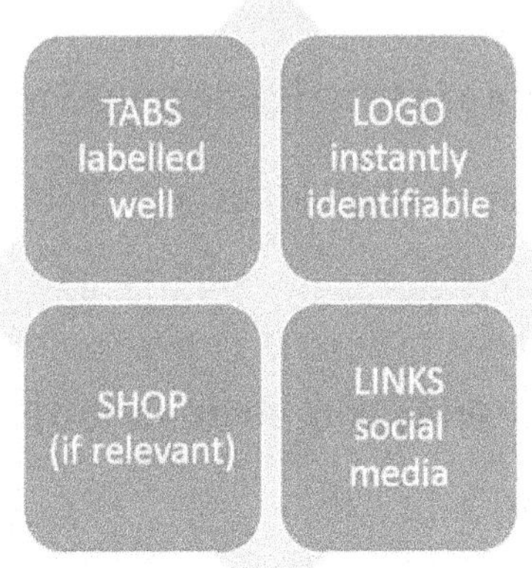

These four elements are important when designing a website. You can use a free website platform: Wordpress and Wix both have free options. I use Wix as it is easier to navigate and the styles are modern. It is also 100 percent safe from viruses. With both options you can buy a domain relatively inexpensively. We have a store that has the added protection of PayPal so I know my customers are doubly safe.

If the prospect of building a website is terrifying for you I would suggest you hire someone. Wix does have these services and no, I am not earning any commission from them for my recommendation.

I recall when I knew nothing about websites and a company who built the website I wrote for were commissioned to add on a page designated to my new venture. They charged $750 for 20 hours' work and the page I was left with was really basic and practically unusable. I discovered the platform I use now and for just over $200 a year I have my own domain, store and heaps of add-on apps that I can use. It is also easy to build and learn how to navigate.

Your website represents you, so dress it well and make sure it says what you want it to say.

# *Illustrators*

If you are publishing a children's book or a book that includes illustrations, it is important to build a relationship with your illustrator. You will be working closely with them, which at times may require pushing boundaries. Mutual respect for each other will help you overcome hurdles if they arise.

When you find an illustrator who draws in the style you like, does the work within the timeframe and is easy to get along with, cherish them, they are worth treasuring. Let them know how much you value them and how grateful you are.

There is a process to illustrating a vision. Below is an example of how My Silly Mum came to be.

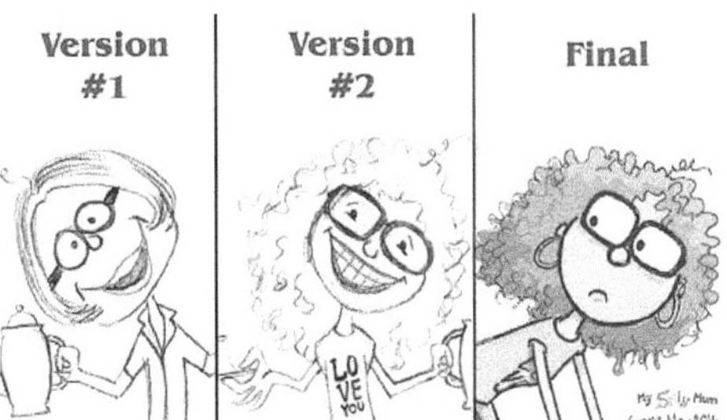


It is hard work but so worth it when you see it all develop into something worthy of commercial distribution.

# *Talks and event bookings*

As you become increasingly more established as an author or publisher you may be invited to do a talk or deliver a workshop. This is a great opportunity to sell books and usually you will get paid. There will be instances when you won't. It is up to you if you pursue them or not. I do as many as possible as it is free marketing for my business and an opportunity for me to build my profile while doing something good.

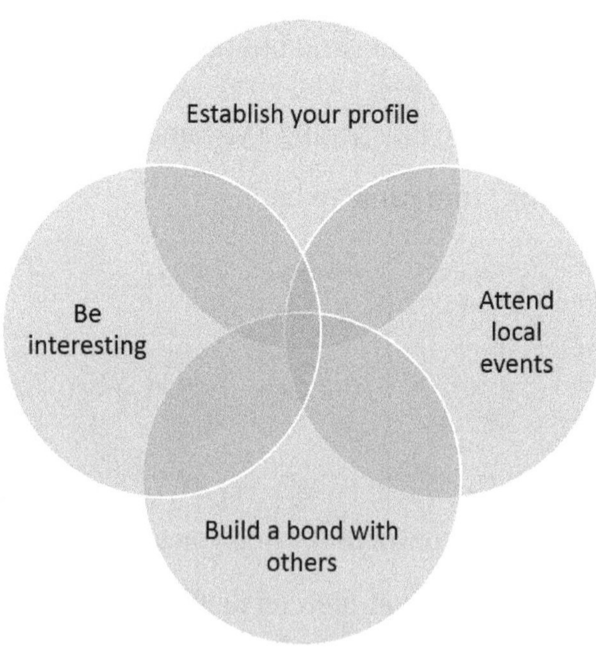

Another option you may consider is creating your own event specific to your area of expertise. My advice is to see through your first event without much expectation, ensuring that you give it your all. This should result in a positive outcome with word of mouth to follow.

Recommendations from others in important circles is imperative to achieve success through events. You will then be able to promote in these circles successfully for future workshops. Keep moving forward and if you discover a winning workshop along the way, stick it out.

# *Awards, reviews and best seller status*

Becoming an award-winning author or business will assist you in increasing your brand profile. Accolades like these help others sit up and take notice of your work. It is important to share these achievements as you gain them, it helps maintain momentum alongside your writing journey.

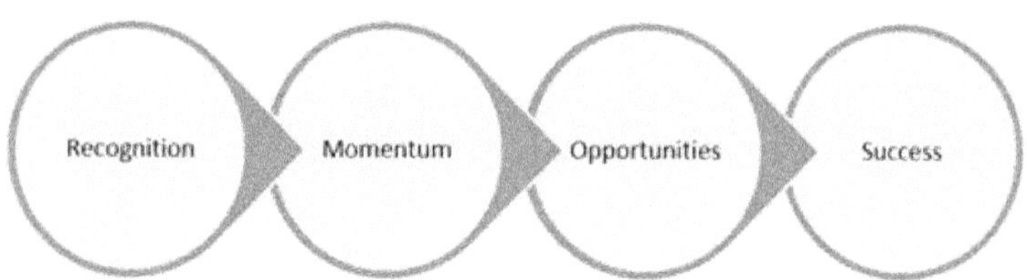


It was through being a finalist in the Ausmumpreneur awards in 2015 that I raised the profile of Serenity Press. A buzz surrounded me and helped me to stand out from the crowd. I embraced the momentum and ran with it. It has been like a snowball running down a hill, continuously growing and gaining momentum. Take time to enter awards that are relevant to you. Be prepared to invest in yourself. Let's face it, being an author is being a small business.

Reviews by influencers i.e. fellow authors, friends, celebrities and influencers to your target audience can make a real difference when promoting a book. Reviews are a sure-fire way to get readers interested in your book. I have witnessed many successes because the right person fell in love with an author's book. It is your job, as the author or publisher, to ensure the book is readily available so that when a wave in sales occurs you are ready to capitalise on it. Such success can also lead to best seller status.

This can be achieved in a few different ways. Through eBook sales via Amazon, selling books in stores and directly. Authors often have a promotion leading up to release day. This is a great opportunity to gain eBook sales that can lead to being number one in your chosen category during release week. There is also that added option of having an eBook pre-order which in turn helps with the spike in sales on release day. Being in Australia helps as Amazon has a designated Kindle site and so sales are gauged on Australian sales and if you have an Australian readership you could be onto a winner. Pursuing awards, reviews and best-selling status can be time consuming, but the rewards are ten-fold when it comes together.

# Social media

Having a social media presence is a must for authors wanting to build a profile. My online presence is very strong. Even if it doesn't reflect on the normal everyday reality of my life, it does showcase my business journey. In turn I have built a network of amazing people who feel that they are part of my journey too, and they are, as they are cheering from the sidelines.

Facebook is a fabulous place to be present when you are in business and an author. I have a rule wherein I block out all negatives and only focus on positives and it works. There are lots of negative people on there but when you adapt this rule from day one, navigating Facebook is a more productive experience. You will need to have a profile and from that an author/business page where you accumulate likes. You can run promotions and showcase on other people's pages to gain likes. Often success is measured by how many likers you have. Many successful businesses have been built upon this platform.

Twitter is not as personal as Facebook and anonymity is more achievable through this platform. It has evolved to be more about business. I have had success through tagging in celebrities and media via Twitter. The key is to have an eye-catching image or headline so that your tweet stands out. Be mindful that your tweet will be seen by many people who know your brand so keep within the perimeters of integrity of your brand.

Instagram has fast become one of the best ways to build a profile. Images talk volumes on this platform. Have a good camera and develop an eye for detail when sharing images. It is a great marketing tool and gaining followers is faster than on Twitter and Facebook.

All-in-all, social media is the way to go if you want to create a genuine following. It is also a wonderful way to reflect back on your journey to success.

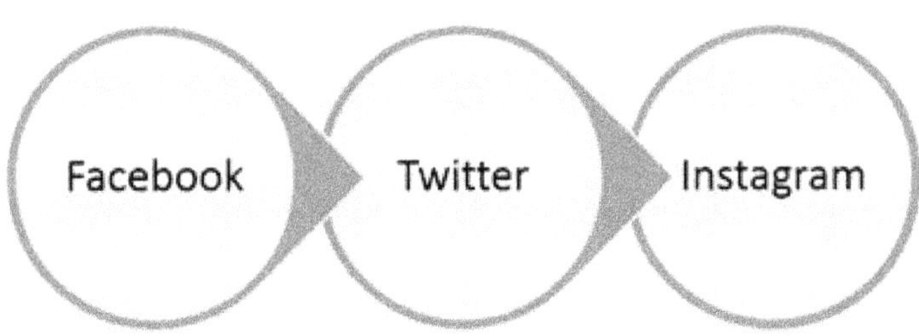

# *Build your database*

Your database is your direct line of contact to potential customers and well worth the effort to compile.

An effective way to build a database is through a newsletter pop up – you know, those annoying things that pop up when you visit a website?

Collect email addresses like gold coins. Each one is worth more.

## ***Collect, collect collect***

# *Financials*

Keeping on top of your finances is imperative if you are to be a successful business. That doesn't mean you have to penny pinch, on the contrary it assists in helping you to invest in your business the right way.

I have learnt this the hard way. For the first few years of business I just collected a pile of receipts in a box and on my computer and when tax time came around I was drowning in a pile of paper.

That is my past and now I have implemented spreadsheets that track income and expenditure. It is very liberating as a business to know where you stand financially. Until I got to this point I felt like I had more of an expensive hobby than a business but now I know that my business has great value.

Quickbooks is an inexpensive resource to use for managing your daily accounts. It even syncs with PayPal and our bank so that everything can be managed together. This is good for my business as a large percentage of our online sales go through PayPal. There are also other resources that come highly recommended by many businesses, including Xero and MYOB. You can also keep your own spreadsheets and your accountant can assist you in managing them.

As you grow it is important to have a structure in place so that you don't have to worry about organising finances and will have financial data at the touch of a button if need be. This is an ideal and a real possibility if you focus energy on building a strong foundation early on.

There are so many other financial considerations, such as funding your business, grants, investing and many other elements. These opportunities will be specific to your business journey. It is important to find a strategy that works for your business, just like I did for mine.

Being confident about your financial position is the key to success. The main goal of business is to be profitable so that should be the main focus.

# *Mindset*

## *Think like a publisher*

A positive go-getting productive mindset is something you can't buy. A productive mindset is where you make the best use of your personal resources. These are your time, your energy and your actions. This means not trying to do everything and be everything. It is more about doing what is right for your business and moving forward accordingly.

Enjoying the process that could be challenging for others but more enjoyable for you because of the positive productive mindset. With a clear, focused goal as the outcome, you can move forward always knowing when to push and when to sit and wait for things to happen. That only comes with being mindful.

Time

Energy

Action

The important elements of a positive productive mindset are:

- Curiosity – This is when you have a willingness to seek and explore and enquire about new ideas and concepts. It is a research stage that is instrumental in progressing. It is the willingness and desire to know and learn new things.

- Desire - Without desire there is nothing to drive us to make progress and improve. Motivation derives from the desire to achieve something.

- Vision – Being able to visualise your goal helps you focus on it and gives you an idea of what the outcome would look like. Ultimately it attracts all of the things you need to come your way as you will be putting-it-out-there, so to speak. With that vision you can accomplish the seemingly impossible.

- Critical thinking – Having the ability to assess a situation in an objective manner means you can be realistic about potential stumbling blocks along the way. I think of it as like risk management. Look at the pros and cons and be willing to make the necessary changes. Even just being aware of the hurdles and preparing for them is a positive.

- Self-confidence - This is knowing that what you are pursuing is achievable and you are confident that you can master it. You will have faith and belief in your capability to achieve what you set out to achieve. With self-confidence and faith, you can reach your full potential and make magic happen for you and your business.

# My Publishing Journey

Looking at my background, publishing books would not have been foreseen in my future. Mind you, nobody could ever have dared to imagine what I would end up doing as I have always embraced opportunity and was always 'going somewhere'. I suppose I have always prepared myself to go that little bit further than anyone else. This has often gotten me into strife. During my teenage years and even during my twenties I found it hard to settle as I pursued exciting opportunity after exciting opportunity. I didn't often stop to think why, I just knew that I was following my heart and if it felt right, I did it. Areas of employment for me ranged from acting on stage, being a presenter, administration, managing a deli, supervising a high risk area in a meat factory and tutoring special needs students in the mental health sector. The list goes on and on and on ...

## *Early days*

I was never good in school; I went to an all-girls convent

secondary school in Ireland. I remember my parents being so proud that I had passed the entrance exam and earnt my place in the most prestigious girls' school in our county. I was very proud too. I was doing well and getting by, but I always found it hard in the classes to hold my interest and I would get bored. I know now that I had made the wrong subject choices. Physics would have been a wonderful science to have under my belt but I never thought I was smart enough to choose it and chose biology like my closer peers. Mistake! Looking back I would have benefited by being more philosophically based in my choices. Mind you, choices were limited as most of the subjects were compulsory.

To cut a long story short, my interests navigated more towards the social side of school and I would often wag classs. At recess and lunch I would be found smoking behind the demountable, cigarettes I got from selling my dinner tickets.

I rolled my skirt up high and I was becoming popular. I liked it, it made me feel good. Said skirt heightening would of course not take place until I was clearly out of view from both home and school.

Not so long ago an old friend from school contacted me

on Facebook and said, 'Imagine if Mr Johns knew that you published your own book.' Mr Johns was my English teacher and he used to make me read out loud in class. I stayed back after class and asked him not to because it made me blush excessively and my mind would go in a tizzy. But he made me anyway so I got up and walked out of the class. That rebellious nature was not tolerated in this school.  It was definitely the beginning of the demise of my educational prospects in secondary school. I couldn't wait to leave, get a job and start earning money.

I got a job in a tights factory checking stockings for holes. It wasn't glamorous but I thought I was the bee's knees earning 62 pounds a week. It didn't last long as the company went into administration. I got a job in my local town in the meat factory. This was my first experience of feeling that I was an integral part of a team and I loved it. Even though the job itself was totally mundane and mind numbing at times, the fun we had as a team and the camaraderie that was connected to it made me clock in every day.

## *Education*

When my son was ready to start school I knew I couldn't do

shift work because lifting him out of bed early on an Irish winter morning was not something I was prepared to do. So I resigned from my supervisory position and went back to school. I worked part-time while doing an access course which earned me acceptance for a place studying media at university, but it was not the right time. I had secured myself a perfect administration job that I enjoyed a lot and would open doors for me that surpassed any expectation I could have imagined.

I chose to study Humanities through an outreach university programme at my local college and I worked hard juggling everything for a few years.

My manager brought to my attention a course that was available through a Dublin college that would require me to attend a weekend workshop in various locations around Ireland for the duration of a year. It was fully funded because it was aimed at training people to go out into the community and break down barriers that had been built up during the troubles in Northern Ireland. I was accepted and oh boy, did I learn so much during this time!

I was then offered a position teaching with a local college in their out centres. It was perfect and the same year I graduated with a Diploma in Humanities through the University of Ulster. I felt like the luckiest woman in the world and I was!

## *Turnaround*

I endured a low time in my life that caused me to look inside. This was something I had never even considered when I was rallying through life at an excessive speed. Everything slowed down and simplified around me, it had to or I couldn't have handled it. Luckily I had worked in the mental health sector, and although I was not a nurse I knew what was happening to my mind and I also knew what I needed to do to get through it. I suppose the main thing was not to fear it! I took each day as it came and focused on my children who needed me.

This time was invaluable in my transition to becoming a more aware person. I looked within and began to see the real Karen who was patiently waiting to make an appearance. I discovered that when we are at a low point it often guides us to a state of contemplation and a quieter place where the craziness of before is past and with a clear mind, positive change can be worked towards.

## *Discovering creativity*

With my new-found appreciation for life I ventured forward at a slower pace, focusing purely on the simple things guided by my heart. We moved to Australia (when I was 35 weeks pregnant with my third child) to set up a new life for our family and when I arrived I felt so inspired. I began writing and illustrating children's books. It made my heart sing and my children loved it. I felt as if my puzzle was coming back together again. I was willing to be patient and go with it, not forcing it like I would have before.

***"Life is not about finding yourself, it is about creating yourself."***

I suppose without even knowing it I was reinventing myself. My son helped me choose the logo Mamma Mac's and I began to make the stories into homemade books. Even though this was not about achievement I decided to send my manuscript to a manuscript assessor called Angel Wings Manuscript Assessment that was based in Melbourne. When the assessment came back it was so encouraging, it was a great feeling. I didn't do anything with it at that time. I just began to share the love of my stories with my new Australian friend and her beautiful girls; she was always so positive when she spoke of my stories and I even created characters for her girls.

As I couldn't afford to send presents to nieces and nephews I would create a character for them, write them a story and do illustrations in their own personal book. As I grew I would computerise the books more. I remember the excitement when I discovered Microsoft Publisher; I could really bring my books to life. When my children were asleep I would sit with my Faber Castell pencils and illustrate pictures for my next book project. I felt free and happy when I did this and seeing my son's face when I produced a new book for him was all the motivation I needed to keep going. I worked on about 30 books over this period in my life.

My husband saw my passion and wanted to support me as he believed in me so when I saw an advertisement in the paper asking, 'Do you want to publish your book, call us,' I did. We went to meet the guy in a coffee shop in Applecross (a fancy suburb in Perth, Western Australia). We had arrived early and so took a walk along the water's edge with our kids. I remember mentioning that if this guy was a rip off I would be able to do it myself someway. So off we went to meet him and he was charming, of course, and to an enthusiastic aspiring author what he had to offer was priceless, my book published and 500 copies to sell. The approximate price he gave me was $8000 and he had papers for me to sign there and then. But something told me not to, it was too much money for my family at the time but I felt that I was wiser for meeting with this guy. It was part of my journey.

I secured a deal with a local children's charity to raise money through the sale of my books. They believed in me and agreed to me putting their name on my books. This was an amazing affirmation for me that others believed in my dream, but time and circumstance didn't align and so I didn't pursue it further. I decided to send my manuscript off to be considered by publishers. I collected a list of submission offices in Australia and I sent my books everywhere. This process takes a very long time and I learnt to be patient. I was very close to an offer of publication with a few of my manuscripts and so I knew that what I was writing was good. Some of the letters I received came with a personal message expressing that the editors loved my work, but that it just didn't fit with their requirements at that time and to please keep submitting.

## *Passion for writing*

I then joined a site called adoptamum.com which was co-created by my beautiful friend. As I was living away from my mum I decided to join. WOW! I was introduced to a more loving metaphysical way of thinking. All of the women on the site shared support and love with one another, it was a virtual sanctuary where we would meet and message each other and we never felt alone. I began to write little things and post them in the groups. I began to write articles on things that inspired me at any given time. I was changing so much at this time and I was absorbing information to support my new-found need for information. I showed some of my articles to the owner of the site and she was excited and asked if I would like to publish them there. They flowed and flowed and the owner published them. I was soon offered the position of 'Resident Writer'. This blew my mind! I was so excited; I couldn't believe that I was classed as a writer, someone who had walked out of her English class. I was given up on and I suppose I had given up on myself in that sense but now ... I had found a burning desire to write, write, write and I discovered that as I wrote I healed a little more.

## *Alignment*

When everything shifts and aligns to make something possible it is quite magical and this is what happened when I chose to write my first novel. I had just given birth to my fourth child and was feeling very inspired. I had been becoming increasingly aware of the signals we are sent from time to time affirming that we are doing the right thing for us. I came across a writing challenge called NaNoWriMo that intrigued me, I had always been a person who excelled when challenged but I hadn't challenged myself in this way for a long time. The urge was there though and although many people would have commented that my timing was not great as I had a newborn, I knew the timing was perfect. I was at home and hey, what else would I be doing while breastfeeding?

What would I write about? The challenge was starting in a few days and I knew that I had to do it but was I being silly even considering it with only a few days to go? Then it happened. I was watching a bit of morning TV (something that I never did) and Whoopi Goldberg said something that resonated with me so deeply. I had experienced a miscarriage a few years previously and had not fully healed. She mentioned that it had been a visitor that came to help shift me back onto the right track in preparation for receiving the real gift. It was a truly big AHA! moment for me and I felt an overwhelming urge to share this message with the world. But how? Then I remembered NaNoWriMo and I knew that it would happen and it did. For 30 days I wrote 1667 words each day to achieve the 50,000 words required to win the challenge. I could not believe how it all flowed together. Every night the kids would go to bed easily and I would sit with my newborn, breastfeed her to sleep with one arm and single-handedly type my way to 50,000 words. The novel was finished; it was an emotional rollercoaster but I DID IT! What now?

## *My first publishing experience*

Okay, so what now? Would I send it to an array of publishers like I did with my children's manuscripts? That didn't sit well with me because I really wanted to bring it to the world now and I didn't want to wait years to have my book in my hand. I shared it with the people I love to get some feedback. My mum is my biggest critic and she absolutely loved it and my closest friend said that it 'just had to be published'. Then it happened, the site I was writing for sponsored the publication of my book. How lucky was I? My dream was becoming a reality.

I sent a self-publishing company my manuscript and the wheels were set in motion. I knew what I wanted for a cover but they told me the final decision was with them as they knew best. I thought this was strange. All was sailing along wonderfully, then I got calls from another department of the publishing house wanting me to get my book edited and it was going to cost more than the publication. This was a whopper, a total dream zapper. So how was this going to happen? I wanted the best for my book but I didn't want it to be changed. I loved my characters and their journeys, but I couldn't have it going out there with my name on it if it wasn't good enough to be read. After much deliberation, and with the support of my hard-working hubby, I chose to have it edited. To be honest I was surprised. I thought they would have changed heaps of it but they didn't, the lady just gently made it more readable.

The publishing company made a booboo and sent the unedited version to eBook format and I received an email from someone who bought it saying they found it hard to read and were finding it even harder to get any satisfactory response from the publisher. I contacted the publisher directly and they were not all that helpful and would not accept any blame. I asked them to reimburse the lady her money and offer her a free copy of the edited book. I still to this day don't know if they did that. They also wanted to charge me extra for different things and I felt it was becoming a real money pit; they didn't care about me or my book! I received phone call after phone call asking me to buy more books at a 'special price', marketing plans at a 'special price' and it went on and on. I received my first royalty letter stating I had sold an amazing five books and the publisher had earnt more royalties on each of these books than I did. It all just seemed so WRONG!

## *The Publishing venture*

But as my quote said in the front of my book:

***'From all negative situations is the potential for a positive outcome.'***

I chose to focus on the positives with my book. I entered it into the Readers' Favourite book awards contest. It received a five-star review and was a finalist in the 2012 awards contest. I built up a rapport with the guys at Readers' Favourite because I believe so much in them. They work tirelessly and they give more than they receive. They do their job for the love of helping authors move forward in their career by making the process easier. They offer heaps of services from proofreading, to reviewing to book trailers etc ... the list is endless.

I had since also completed my second novel and things were exciting for me as an author. I noticed that affirmations were coming from all around letting me know I was doing the right thing. Being an author and selling books can be a full-time job so I researched what works and what doesn't and began to identify who was real and who wasn't. There are many people out there in the writing business who give more than they take in financial gain; to have a connection with people like this is priceless.

One of my friends from Buildingbeautifulbonds.com approached me early in 2011 and asked if I thought it would be possible to publish books. She was a fan of my work and I had mentored her to write her life story, 'In Search of My Soul'. After some research I discovered that the publishing company I had hired to publish my book used services that I could use myself and I could have complete control of my own book and royalties. Instead of earning $2 a book commission I could print my book for $4 to $5 and keep the rest for myself.

After a lot of work and research I worked it all out. I discovered that the US-based Ingram company Lightning Source had recently set up an office in Melbourne (Time + Circumstance = Magic). I had nothing to lose and so I applied to Lightning

Source to open an account as a publisher. This was what we needed as it provided us with access to worldwide distribution and we could print as few or as many books as we wanted. We could also place overseas orders by using their printing houses in both the UK and the US.

We were accepted as a publisher and we affiliated with Buildingbeautifulbonds.com who supported us and believed in us so much. As soon as we put up our logo a book submission came through with a truly inspirational story. Our vision was to publish inspirational stories so we had it edited and published Prickle in a Dream within a month and have not stopped since.

## *Guided*

From the outset I was guided through each step of the way. If I had thought of every step as a whole picture we would have been totally overwhelmed and run away. Instead I chose to take one step at a time and every challenge was an opportunity to learn and grow and oh boy, I love to learn new things.

I discovered my absolute passion for creating books. When one of our authors sends me a signed copy of their book thanking me for helping them make their dream become a reality, I beam with immense joy that I have been a positive influence on their publishing journey

Little achievements came along at exactly the right time to affirm that I was on the right path with Serenity Press. A few of these to date are:

- In 2012, I was awarded acceptance into Stanford's Who's Who.
- In 2013, I was asked to be part of my first Perth-based weekend conference alongside Andrew Jobling.
- In 2014, Serenity Press was accepted as a publisher by APA.
- In 2014, we began our transition to becoming a traditional publisher.
- In 2015, I was a finalist in the Business Excellence category of Ausmumpreneur.
- In 2015, the wonderful Monique Mulligan joined our team. Her expertise is exceptional.
- In 2015, we had the most successful launch of our first romance anthology Rocky Romance at the inaugural Rockingham Writers Centre Book Fair.
- In 2015, we were given permission to gift Oprah a Serenity Press gift basket when she came to visit Perth.
- In 2016, I became an Ausmumpreneur Writing and

Publishing expert, Ausmumpreneur Perth Ambassador and MC at their 2016 conference.

- We will continue to grow, think outside the box, support Australian authors and grow a strong Serenity Press team.

- 2016 was our greatest year of successes and we became a company.

## *Attraction*

I have used the universal Law of Attraction to bring to me exactly what it is that I want to experience in my lifetime. I am so convinced that we all have the power to create anything that we want into our lives and when we connect this power to following our heart's desire, magic will happen! I decided to put my study cap on again and I earnt myself a certification as an advanced Law of Attraction practitioner. I have learnt that we are the only ones who limit ourselves. I apply this to my business principle and it allows Serenity Press to grow, albeit unconventionally, but most definitely with passion and determination.

***"Where there is a will there is always a way."***

I have always lived by this motto and now with my new-found appreciation for life I use it to be the best I can possibly be!

# *Conclusion*

The Serenity Press initial vision was to share as many inspirational stories with the world as we possibly can but this has been further enhanced by offering authors the opportunity to publish their books in a positive way. It has now evolved further to become a traditional publishing company who creates amazing opportunities for authors.

We have created Making Magic Happen for authors who prefer to follow the self-publishing route and I am passionate that our authors will never feel negative about their book. Your book publishing experience deserves to be a positive one.

I have always known Serenity Press would be an inspirational story in itself; I know this because we have the truest of intention with every endeavour we undertake. We have made affiliations with wonderful people and the only way is up for us. We are a publisher with heart and as we grow, our authors grow too. We are a family and I am proud of what we continually achieve with our wonderful authors.

*What's your publishing journey so far?*

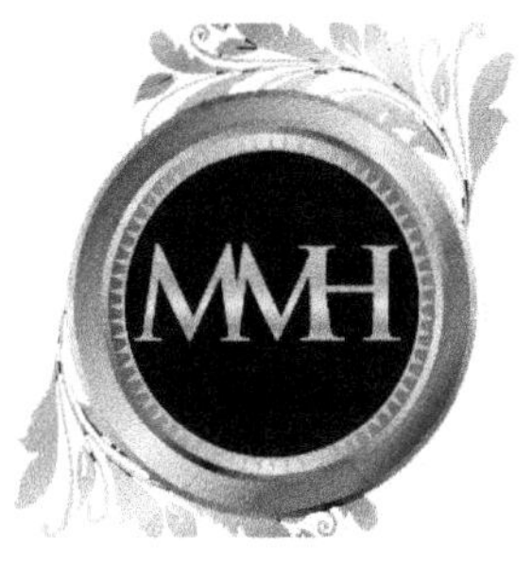
MMH



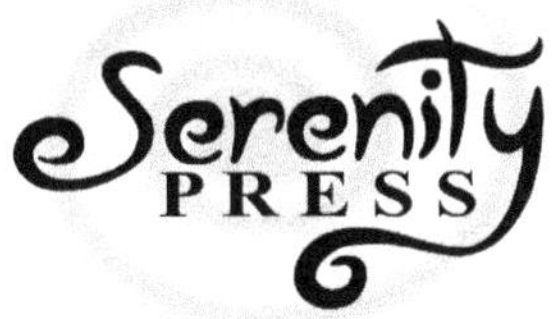
Serenity
PRESS



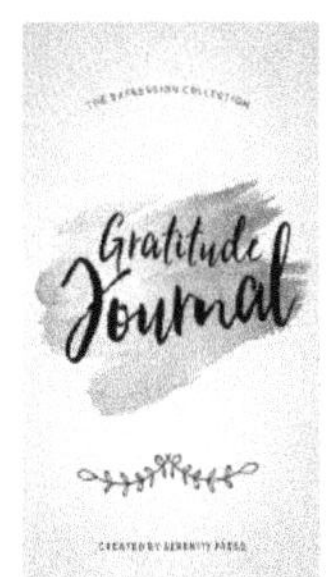
Gratitude
Journal

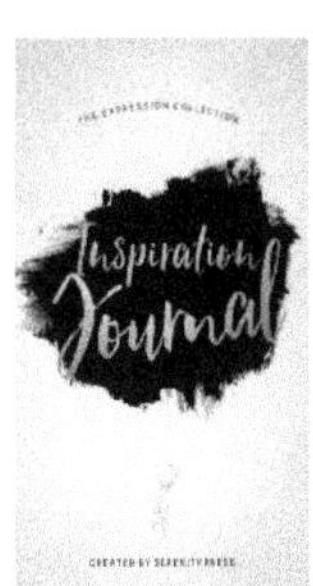
Inspiration
Journal

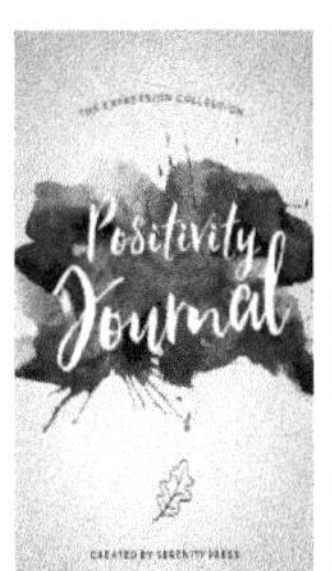
Positivity
Journal

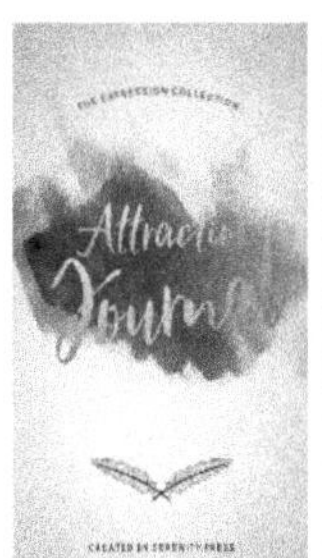

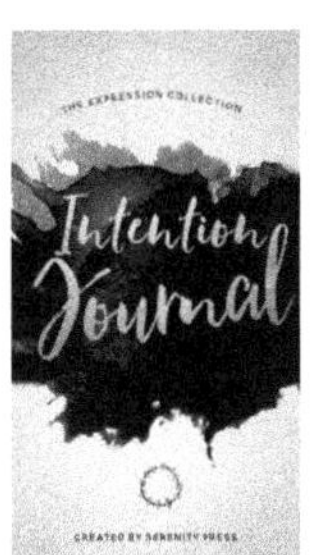
Intention
Journal

www.ingramcontent.com/pod-product-compliance
Ingram Content Group UK Ltd.
Pitfield, Milton Keynes, MK11 3LW, UK
UKHW020135250726
13967UKWH00002B/671